Confessions of a Tax Accountant

Outrageous, Hilarious and Totally True Stories

Noelle Allen, C.P.A.

Confessions of a Tax Accountant

Copyright © 1993 Canyon View Institute

Library of Congress Catalog Card Number 93-73123

Allen, Noelle

1. Humor I. Title

ISBN 1-884221-00-9

Cartoons by Will S. Coleman

First Edition, Second Printing

Printed in the United States of America

CONTENTS

Introduction 9

THE AUDIT LOTTERY

Fear and Trembling 20

The Plain Facts 21

A Little History 22

It's In The Book 24

"Seeing Is Believing" 27

Producing The Evidence 30

"Crime and Punishment" 31

TO BE MARRIED OR NOT TO BE MARRIED —THAT IS THE QUESTION!

The Pseudo-Bride 37

The Tainted Spouse 39

Only In California 43

The Divorce Vacation 47

WHAT ABOUT TAX SHELTERS?

The Pregnant Cow 50

They Fly By Night 52

The Spoils 54

Phantom Income 56

CHEATING ON YOUR INCOME TAX AND OTHER GAMES OF CHANCE

The Rationalizer 59
The Parking Lot Gambler 60
Robbing Peter to Pay Paul 62
Police Brutality? 63
The Old Lady Who Lived In The Shoe 66
What's In A Name! 68

A FEW OF MY FAVORITE DEDUCTIONS

The Spouting Cupids 72
The Well-endowed Girlfriend 76
The Collection Plate 79
Valuable Junk 81

The African Artifact 84
Once A Mother, Always A Mother 86
A Fishy Story 88
Ancient Greece 91

MONKEY BUSINESS

The Case of The Disappearing Dogs 95
Tax Talk 96
Tax Deductible Child Birth 97
The Human Doughnut Machine 98
"The Bluebird of Happiness" 100
"The Workaholic CPA" 103
The Little Business That Could 105
Are We Having Fun Yet? 108

The Barefoot Stockbroker 110
The "Racy Dentist" 112

BORN FREE, TAXED TO DEATH
Florida Sunset 114
"War and Peace" 117

UNDER THE GREEN EYESHADE
My Clients—It Takes All Sorts 121
Tax Revenge of The Wronged Spouse 124
The Handicapped Golfer 127
The Accountant's Ego 129
The Referral 132
A Final Word 135

DEDICATION

I gratefully dedicate this book to U.S. taxpayers. It is absolutely true to say that without their help, often unwitting, I could not have written it.

INTRODUCTION

The story of my becoming a CPA testifies to the serendipity in life.

I went to college in the 1960s, and in those days women didn't major in business or accounting. It just wasn't the "done" thing. So I majored in Psychology. As a result of that choice, when I graduated from college, I had two job offers. One was to go to work for United Air Lines as a stewardess—that's what they called "flight attendants" then. The other was to work for the IRS as a tax auditor. I joined the IRS because it didn't insist that I lose 12 pounds! I'm a tax accountant today because I had a sweet tooth that was particularly keen on hot fudge sundaes.

Introduction

However, in the end, tax law appealed to me. I liked its complexities and the fact that it was always changing. Eventually, I became a CPA and went into tax practice because I liked it. Little did I know how useful my psychology degree would be in my profession! Over the years, I've found that once people tell me about their finances in the process of tax preparation, they think they can tell me everything. Including what's too personal to reveal to their therapists!

One of my friends who's a marriage counselor recently told me that in one of her counseling sessions, after a couple had related to her every intimate detail of their sex life, she then asked about their finances. With shock registering in her eyes, the wife looked at her and said very coldly, *"That's* a very private matter."

Introduction

I sometimes find myself occupying a unique position in my clients' lives. Sometimes I believe that I play a bigger role in their lives by doing their taxes than I would have played had I become a psychologist. Tax law may be "impersonal"; practicing it is anything but!

There's another myth I'd like to put to rest: CPAs are dull. We're viewed as "bean counters" who wear green eyeshades! My experiences in the business have led me to an opposite view, when it comes to tax accountants. In fact, those of us "under the green eyeshade" know secrets and stories that have something to do with numbers, but far more to do with human nature and how men and women deal with one of the inevitabilities of life—**TAXES**.

First, let's talk about tax in general. To most people, "tax" is a negative word, and when mentioned in connection with the GOVERNMENT, it becomes a double negative! It has

Introduction

taken me many years to understand just how much people *hate* paying taxes and *hate* everything connected with paying taxes, i.e., the IRS, Form 1040, April 15th—and, sometimes, CPAs! Since my entire professional life has been bound up with income tax, however, I am personally not intimidated by the concept or by those who enforce tax law. It has come as a slow revelation to me that most people feel very differently.

"Fear" and "intimidation" are two of the words most associated with income tax. In fact, I've found that people who are *not* frightened by taxes or the IRS are often liberated from anxiety simply because they have decided not to participate in the "voluntary compliance" system that we have in America. In short, they're not worried because they plan to try to cheat the IRS! (Note: This is why a voluntary system is most effective when it is *least* voluntary). Over the last twenty-five years, all types of people have been my clients—timid, aggressive, assertive, or "creative."

Introduction

In recent years, clients have become more hostile about taxes because taxes have become so complex. People find themselves forced to have their taxes prepared for them by experts, because it takes them too much time or is too frustrating to do their own. This despite IRS low-ball estimates of how long it takes to prepare certain forms!

Given how my clients feel about taxes, I find myself about as popular as a car repair mechanic or a dentist. I'm seen as a "necessary evil." Many people feel the same way sitting in my waiting room to see me as they do in their dentist's office. It's just that painful!

But can people hope to avoid us? As long as you have teeth, you'll see a dentist. And as long as you pay taxes, CPAs will be around. And every time a new tax bill passes, I must admit that it's fair to call it "The Accountants' Full-Employment Act." New tax law *does* stimulate business for us

Introduction

until the new twists are unraveled—and even beyond, if it's complex enough. You may find it comforting to know that even accountants must struggle with new laws.

Recently, I heard repeated a conversation between the Chief Financial Officer of a major oil company and a high-ranking executive of the American Institute of CPAs. The CFO was telling the CPA that he was heaving a large sigh of relief because he had just recently filed for his oil company its current corporate income tax return, which had taken 21 employees an entire year to prepare and twelve Mayflower moving boxes to transport the paperwork to the IRS, and the only thing he knew for sure was that the tax return was probably *wrong*!

The Internal Revenue Code is certainly a fine example of "Why belabor the necessary when the irrelevant is available?"

Introduction

And, yes, "tax simplification" is an oxymoron right up there with "airline food" and the "postal service."

In addition to the complexity inherent in tax law, the plot is further thickened by politics—which is part of the reason for the complexity in the first place. Taxes are an *art*, not a science. As a famous French philosopher once said, "The art of taxation is similar to the art of plucking a goose. You are successful by plucking the greatest amount of feathers with the least amount of squawking."

Enter stage right, the special interest groups; and on stage left, Congress. And the denouement? Tax law being made is a little like sausage being made—and you wouldn't want to watch!

This book consists mostly of cases I've come up against in my own practice, first as an IRS auditor and all the years since as a CPA. A few anecdotes have been passed on to me by accountant colleagues. In addition, there are two or three stories that come from tax court cases that are part of the public record.

While these stories are true, details have been changed to protect the innocent, the guilty, and, of course, myself!

As you read these confessions, some of you may find yourself thinking—if only momentarily—"Aha, what a great idea! If only I'd thought of that!" While I wrote this book to amuse rather than instruct I expect that many readers will not only marvel at the peccadilloes of their fellow taxpayer but learn some tax law that may prove helpful to them.

While it should be unnecessary to do so, I feel compelled to state that I do not in any way recommend adopting any of the strategies for cheating the IRS that some of my "creative" and occasionally—*very occasionally*—ignorant clients have attempted. To be perfectly clear: *I advise against cheating.*

Introduction

Now, some of you are wondering, "Isn't that precisely why some people seek out the expertise of CPAs come tax time? Not for help in cheating, of course, but to reduce their taxes?" Of course they do—and with good reason! Just keep in mind that while a CPA's calculations may often result in a tax lower than the one you arrive at, CPAs have an obligation both to their clients and to themselves to abide by tax laws. We are bound by a code of ethics promulgated by our profession and Circular 230, a code of ethics which the Internal Revenue Service enforces for attorneys, CPAs, and Enrolled Agents. We look to our clients to provide us with accurate and truthful information. In my own tax practice, if I suspect that what a client tells me may not be true, I ask some probing questions. In a few instances, the client's answers have made all too clear an intent to defraud—and I then make clear my unwillingness to proceed on a fraudulent return.

I have had to ask a couple of would-be clients to leave my offices. But while CPAs must have a reasonable basis for claiming exemptions and deductions, it's not up to us to wrest the truth from our clients—the IRS will do that, if it suspects that it requires doing!

Nevertheless, there's no question that taxpayers' desire to part with as little as possible of their money to the IRS has been responsible for my hearing the fascinating confessions of this book.

About the Author: Noelle Allen, CPA, began her career as an IRS office auditor working in San Francisco. She later went into private practice and has been a practicing CPA for more than 20 years. Her company in Cupertino, California has 800 individual tax clients ranging from CEO's of companies to retired pensioners. She is a member of the California CPA Society and the American Institute of CPA's.

THE AUDIT LOTTERY

Fear and Trembling

Fear and trembling are associated with most communications from the IRS. I must admit that even when I see an envelope in my mailbox with an ominous return address such as the "INTERNAL REVENUE SERVICE," my heart beats faster.

Just the other day, a client called to tell me that she had received a communication from the IRS. I asked her what it said. She replied, "I don't know. I'm afraid to open it!" I understood her reaction all too well! Another client, a businessman who received notice of an impending audit, admitted, "I experienced fear, anger, betrayal and, finally, acceptance." These are the emotions that Elisabeth Kubler-Ross identifies with *dying*!

The Plain Facts

In today's world, most individual taxpayers do not receive "eyeball to eyeball" audits. Fewer than 1% of 1040 returns are audited nationwide by live auditors. Many more taxpayers *do* receive from the IRS computer audits that are generated from IRS computer matching programs. For example, the IRS matches all income items reported to it with what has been reported on the tax return. If there is a discrepancy, the IRS then sends a form called a CP-2000 to the taxpayer. (I think they call the form a "CP-2000" because it's about 2,000 pages long). The CP-2000 asks the taxpayer why the income item has not been reported. The IRS collects most tax deficiencies from individual taxpayers in this manner.

A Little History

When I worked for the IRS over 20 years ago, procedures for selecting returns for audit were quite different than they are today. There were no computers to look at returns and make judgment calls about whether they should be classified for audit. Back then, we auditors sat in a long drafty room looking at batches of one hundred returns at a time. We mostly looked for unusual or large deductions. Some people would send in their tax returns on toilet paper, and some would drip blood across the front page. Despite this occasional drama, I became bored with this kind of work quite easily and looked for celebrities' tax returns!

Today, of course, the computer program called "DIF" (discriminant function) chooses returns for audits by "scoring" them. The scores are based on ratios of various deductions to income shown on the return. Exactly what these ratios are is understandably a closely held secret of the IRS. After a return is computer scored, if it has a sufficiently high DIF score, it is dumped out for further review. At this point, a real person looks at the form to determine whether or not it really should be audited up close and personal.

If you lose the audit lottery and actually get a letter from the IRS with the dreaded news of an audit, I have some helpful hints to offer you. One you might consider is to try to schedule your audit for late on a Friday afternoon, preferably just before a three-day weekend! Failing that scheduling success, try keeping good records. Accurate and *complete* record-keeping is your first-line defense in an IRS audit.

It's In The Book

When I was an IRS office auditor, a taxpayer who was a long-distance truck driver—and, fortunately, not my victim—was audited on his travel expenses. When he appeared for the audit, he had the most beautiful records! In fact, his records were so beautiful that the auditor commented on them. When complimented on their neatness, the truck driver smilingly responded, "Of course, these records are beautiful! They should be, because my employer keeps an impeccable file of receipts for all of us to use when we get audited." Second helpful hint regarding audits: Never volunteer any information to an IRS auditor!

Then there was the airline pilot. He was also audited on his away-from-home-expenses. He appeared for his audit with a diary that could be bought at any office supply or

Confessions of a Tax Accountant

stationery store and that he said he'd used to keep track of his daily expenses, including costs for meals, lodging, and incidental expenses. Note: The IRS is usually about two years behind in its audits, so the pilot brought a diary that he said he'd kept on a daily basis for the year in question, two years back. His fatal error: the copyright notation printed on the first page of his expense book was for the current year! The pilot had purchased the book the week before his audit and, using different kinds of ink, had tried to make it look like one that had been kept properly on a daily basis.

By the way, the two IRS clients just described not only had to pay additional taxes but were prosecuted for fraud. Needless to say, their techniques are not recommended or endorsed by this author!

"Seeing Is Believing"

My third helpful hint for handling an audit: Remember, IRS agents are human, too. Play to their humanity and vulnerability, as did one memorable taxpayer-client of mine.

The lady was a third-grade school teacher. In the old days (but not now), taxpayers were sometimes able to deduct travel expense when travel was undertaken for educational reasons. We referred to this deduction as "travel as a form of education." As you might imagine, most people like to claim travel expenses. Anytime you can have fun *and* get a tax deduction, too, you have a "win/win" situation. My third-grade teacher taught South American studies as a part of her social studies unit. One summer vacation, she traveled to South America to observe first-hand what she taught back home. She deducted the expense on that year's tax return—and bought herself an audit lottery ticket! She lost.

Undaunted, however, as she felt that she was right, she appeared for her day in court—an appointment with me. (Note also, *and note well*, that taxpayers are presumed guilty until they prove themselves innocent!). The teacher therefore arrived for her interview armed to the teeth with verification of the trip. This consisted of a slide projector and **500** slides. It seemed to me at the time (and even more so with the advantage of 28 years of hindsight) that it was the better part of valor to allow her the trip deduction. This assessment was seconded by my supervisor—who didn't want to look at 500 slides, either!

Producing The Evidence

Unlike my nice school teacher, many taxpayers can be nasty. They truly resent the IRS and its bureaucratic intrusion into their lives. Even today, one incident remains quite vivid. A taxpayer from the Central Valley of California had mailed a box of records to the IRS for a mail-in audit. The box was not opened right away, and after three or four days, it began to give off a strange and not pleasant odor. Finally, the postal inspector was called to open the package. Inside were a bunch of dead chinchillas. The Central Valley farmer had a chinchilla ranch and had claimed a large loss for the year in question. To verify his losses, he sent the evidence.

Although the farmer claimed to have lost *several hundred* chinchillas, the IRS deemed the whiff of proof sufficient and deemed unnecessary the receipt of the complete remains.

"Crime and Punishment"

You've heard the expression "Crime does not pay." I sometimes think it should be amended to read "Crime does pay, but only after taxes." Many criminals on whom the government cannot obtain sufficient evidence for a conviction for, say, murder or robbery, including Mafia members, have been convicted for tax evasion. Income tax evasion was what finally brought down Al Capone.

The IRS loves to find taxpayers who don't report all their income and then string them up as examples for all the rest of us to see. Now, many people who do not report all their income aren't simply trying to avoid paying taxes but have other compelling reasons for not doing so. They may be engaged in criminal activity of one sort or another. Can you imagine having to write in the 1040 occupation box: "Drug Dealer," " Prostitute," "Armed Robber?"

One case I'll never forget from my long-ago IRS days is how the fraud unit (Criminal Investigation Department) zeroed in on one poor prostitute and got her to report all her income. One ploy of tax evaders is to report *some* of their income, just not *all* of it. This particular "lady-of-the-night" had been paying some tax, but the fraud unit felt that she was substantially under-reporting her income. In order to get her to pay up on the full amount of her earnings, they needed to figure out a foolproof method of reconstructing her income. First, they managed to identify the establishment where she had her laundry done. Over a period of several weeks, the IRS did a count of the number of towels she processed through the laundry, figuring one towel per "customer." After giving her credit for her own personal use of towels, they proceeded to gross up her income based on the number of towels processed and presented her with a revised tax bill. This was truly a case of having one's dirty laundry aired—*and taxed!*

Confessions of a Tax Accountant

TO BE MARRIED OR NOT TO BE MARRIED —THAT IS THE QUESTION!

In the 1990s, this country has seen a return to the importance of family values. Unfortunately, our tax law as currently written does not support or promote marriage. Instead, it supports "living in sin." In fact, the Census Bureau several years ago came up with an acronym for the family unit that is becoming more and more common in the United States: POSSLQ. This stands for "Persons of the Opposite Sex Sharing Living Quarters." The question isn't whether to be married or not to be married, but "What price commitment?"

The Pseudo-Bride

Confessions of a Tax Accountant

Several years ago, one couple came to see me about the tax consequences of tying the knot. Whether they would marry would depend on what I told them. They were content with the status quo—living in sin. But Mr. J's ex-wife didn't like her children visiting a "den of iniquity," and Miss A's mother wanted her daughter married off. So Miss A and Mr. J were considering giving in to these pressures and marrying. Their question to me: How much difference in their taxes between getting married and remaining single? My answer: $2,000 more per annum to be married at their current level of income. Their conclusion: Not to get married but to *pretend* to get married. This they proceeded to do. They hired a catering hall for the reception, and they had a ceremony in a church. Only I, their minister, and, eventually, the IRS knew the truth. By the way, the first year's tax saving paid for the non-wedding.

The Tainted Spouse

If you're over age 55, selling a home can result in a large tax savings. The IRS grants a one-time-only $125,000 exclusion of gain—and a single person gets the same amount as a couple filing a joint tax return. So, if you and your spouse own a house and have been considering divorce, be sure to divorce first, then sell! If you are divorced before the house sells, *both spouses* are eligible for the $125,000 exclusion on their single returns. If the capital gain on your home is substantially higher than $125,000, this would result in a significant tax savings! At the current federal capital gains rate, the savings on the maximum exclusion is $35,000.

For example, let's say that when Bob and Mary started out they bought a home for $250,000. Twenty years later when they decide to go their separate ways, their house has appreciated in value to be worth $600,000! If they sell it, this leaves them with a capital gain of $350,000 less their one-time exclusion of $125,000—which still leaves a capital gain of $225,000 on which they'll have to pay tax. However, if they divorce *before* they sell their house, *both* Bob and Mary qualify for the exclusion. So assuming that they split the capital gain and each assume $175,000 of it, each of them can now take advantage of the exclusion, reducing *each portion* by $125,000—and leaving only $50,000 for each of them liable for capital gains tax! This is just one of the reasons why an "amicable divorce" is so much less expensive than a nasty one!

But watch out when as a couple on a joint return, you use the exclusion. After you've taken the exclusion, you are now a "Tainted Spouse." You can use the exclusion only once. If something should happen to one spouse after using the exclusion, such as death or divorce, the remaining spouse is

Confessions of a Tax Accountant

now "tainted" and cannot remarry and use it again—even if the new spouse has not used the exclusion. This is why in the *Palm Desert News* in Southern California, you can occasionally see classified ads for "attractive middle-aged widower looking for marriage-minded widow, who has not used her over aged-55 exclusion." Caveat for middle-aged dating: interview prospective spouses for over aged-55 exclusion usage.

Usually, the sale of a personal residence is one of the remaining "tax bennies" for middle America. You can either defer your profit by buying a more expensive house or—if you're over age 55—you can use the $125,000 exclusion. But selling a personal residence can be a problem if there has been a divorce situation. Deferring the whole profit means that both spouses have to buy a house that costs more than 50% of the sales price of the one sold. Often, one or both of the spouses cannot afford to do so—especially if they're now on their own.

Consider my clients, Mr. and Mrs. M. They sold their California home in a posh suburb for $650,000. They had lived in it for many years and their profit was $600,000 when they sold it. Initially, there was no problem as they bought another house in another posh suburb for $2,000,000—and deferred their entire profit. But shortly thereafter, marital trouble developed and the M's wanted a divorce. If they sold their two million dollar house and did not re-invest at least one million dollars each, they would have to pay tax on their $600,000 profit from the first house. Since they could not afford to do this, they seemed stuck . . .

One thing about two million dollar houses—they *are* large! This one boasted 6,000 square feet! So Mrs. M simply packed up all her belongings and moved across the house to the guest suite, while Mr. M held the fort in the master bedroom. They became separated under the same roof in order to save the tax on the sale of their home.

They came to see me for a consultation on this thorny problem, to see if I had any brilliant ideas they had not thought of. I didn't.

As Mr. M was leaving to go back to work, Mrs. M asked him to be sure to be home for dinner by 7:30. I looked at her askance and after Mr. M had left, I asked her, "You're still cooking dinner for him?" "Oh," she said, "He and Charlotte—she lives with him in the master bedroom—and Jeff and I—he lives with me in the guest suite—get together in the dining room for dinner and bridge twice a week."

The Divorce Vacation

Several years ago, a Maryland couple found a creative way of dealing with the married vs. single surcharge. (Note: marital status in tax law is determined on the last day of the taxable year: if you're married on December 31, the IRS treats you as if you were married for the whole year. If divorced on December 31, you'll mark the "Single" box to indicate tax status). Our Maryland couple took advantage of this rule by taking a vacation to the Caribbean each year after Christmas. By December 31, they would be divorced and therefore enjoy single tax status for the whole year. Their tax savings paid for their vacation, and after they returned home, they'd remarry in January.

This procedure went very smoothly— and most enjoyably—until they appeared on "Sixty Minutes." Soon after their appearance, they found out that the IRS watches television, too! They were speedily audited, and it was determined by the IRS that their divorce/re-marriage each year was a "sham transaction" and therefore they were not *really* divorced on the last day of the tax year in question and consequently had been underpaying their taxes for some time.

Yes, the IRS made them pay up not only that year, but for all their previous "free" honeymoons. But you know what I think? Married or "single," that was one couple who made teamwork count. Still, I cannot recommend tax evasion as a way for couples to keep their marriages alive....

WHAT ABOUT TAX SHELTERS?

Tax planning in the '90s has become fairly routine because so many so-called "loopholes" were closed with the passage of the 1986 Tax Reform Act. I remember the old days, though, when tax shelters abounded in the land . . .

The Pregnant Cow

When I talk about a tax shelter, I mean, very simply, an investment which created large tax deductions. It could have been an investment in just about anything—gas or oil, real estate, equipment leasing, etc. It really didn't matter. There was something for everybody. How about a calf-breeding operation involving cow eggs and bull sperm inserted into cheap cows. **VOILA**! an expensive calf—and a big write-off!

Confessions of a Tax Accountant

They Fly By Night

One of my clients told me that in the years when tax shelters were the "in thing," tax shelter salesmen were passing him around. He realized that he was a real tax-shelter addict when he got a call on New Year's Eve—the last chance to buy a tax shelter for the year—from a guy who wanted to come to his home and sell him a deal that involved refrigerated railroad cars. He told the guy that he could be interested, but he preferred to see him at his office. The shelter seller said, "What office? I'm in a phone booth." The go-go era for tax shelters provided the perfect climate for the proverbial "fly-by-night" salesperson.

The Spoils

The economics of the shelters went something like this: What people did was to dump a bunch of money into a shelter. Its typical form was something called a "limited partnership" and investors didn't care if they ever saw the money again, because for every dollar they invested, they were getting anywhere from a 4-to-1 to a 10-to-1 write-off on their income tax.

For example: One dairy partnership I saw in the late '70s required a $5,000 investment. The client got to write off $25,000 on his tax return for the $5,000 investment (5-to-1 write-off). Since the highest marginal tax rate in the late '70s could be as high as 50%, it was actually possible to save $12,500 in tax with a $5,000 investment. It doesn't take a rocket scientist to see that you could actually make a profit on the tax savings, so who cared if you ever saw your original $5,000 again—although that would have been nice. But let's not get greedy . . .

Confessions of a Tax Accountant

Phantom Income

Naturally, people flocked to these investments, until the IRS and Congress administered a death blow by calling for massive audits of these partnerships and the Tax Reform Act of 1986 nailed the coffin shut.

Nowadays, we're back to doing tax planning by first evaluating whether the investment is any good first and worrying about taxes later, which is what should have been happening all along. However, tax professionals across the land are still trying to help clients clean up these old messes from what we now call "Burned-out Partnerships" (i.e. the benefits are gone). To add insult to injury, many of them are now throwing off what is called "Phantom Income." That's income the client has to pay tax on, but that he didn't get! Very aptly named, don't you think?

CHEATING ON YOUR INCOME TAX AND OTHER GAMES OF CHANCE

I was called for jury duty recently. As a part of the process of jury selection, the prosecuting attorney in the case asked me if I thought I could tell when someone was lying.

I replied, "Sir, I'm a tax accountant. People lie to me all the time."

His response: "Ms. Allen, you're excused." Note: Great way to get out of jury duty.

The Rationalizer

Consider also the client who bought a computer for her desk-top publishing business. She listed the cost as $3,200, which I deducted. When she was audited on that year's income tax return, I asked for her cancelled check to verify the expense to the IRS. She said that she "sorta" had a cancelled check. I inquired as to how you "sorta have a cancelled check"——-Did the dog eat it? as in the proverbial homework excuse? No. She had a check, but it was for *$1,800*, not $3,200. You see, she'd gotten a deal on the computer. It was *really* worth $3,200, so that's what she deducted!

Confessions of a Tax Accountant

The Parking-Lot Gambler

Yes, people lie to me and try to cheat on their income tax in a variety of different ways. Some favorite examples: One client of mine had six kids and a slew of rental properties. One of the six kids grew up and became my client, too. He told me that he remembered his father routinely gathering all the kids together on Saturday mornings for a trip to the hardware store. He would then disperse the kids into the parking lot to pick up abandoned receipts. The kids got ten cents for each receipt they found. His father would then use the receipts as his back-up in case he was audited about the deductions he'd taken for expenses on his rental properties.

A variation on this theme is to buy a new refrigerator or other significant household purchase such as carpeting for your own personal residence and then claim it as an expense for your rental property.

Robbing Peter to Pay Paul

When asked how many total miles he had on his auto for business, one client was very vague even about how many *total* miles he'd clocked on his auto. His business miles were a complete mystery. Since he was my last client of the evening, I offered to accompany him to his car to check out his odometer. He was then forced to confess that he had disconnected the odometer! You see, the auto was leased and he'd been putting too many miles on the car to get a good deal from the leasing company when his lease was up. Talk about being caught between a rock and a hard place!

Police Brutality?

A great way clients try to lie to me is not to tell me all of their income. In recent years, this has become harder and harder, because most peoples' income is reported on Form 1099 or W-2s. However, there is no requirement to report income to the IRS if the income is less than $600. But that doesn't mean that the income is non-taxable, just that there is no *reporting* requirement. *All earnings are taxable.*

One of my clients is a police officer. Presumably, his job is to uphold law and order and catch criminals—*people who break the law.* Note: it will immediately become apparent here that cheating on one's income tax is not perceived by the general public, including those in law enforcement, to be breaking the law in any traditional sense. Evidently, stealing from the government is really more a "sport," not a *criminal* activity.

In addition to his regular duties, my police officer client moonlighted. He had several part-time jobs as a security guard. In none of these extra jobs did he make more than $600, so no 1099s were sent to the IRS. The policeman came to me and said that his buddies down at the department told him that if you're real careful not to work for any outfit long enough to make over $600 and therefore get a 1099, then you don't have to report the income on your tax return. This thinking is along the same lines as "If a tree falls in the forest and nobody's there, then it doesn't make any noise."

Confessions of a Tax Accountant

Confessions of a Tax Accountant

The Old Lady Who Lived In The Shoe

Another area in which it has become more difficult but still not impossible to abuse the law is claiming false dependency exemptions on tax returns. Several years ago, the IRS began requiring that social security numbers be reported for dependents over 5 years of age. The first year that this was required, seven million dependents disappeared from 1040 tax returns! Since no nationwide natural disaster could account for this phenomenon, the IRS lowered the social security requirement to dependents one year of age and older. And these days, Social Security offices are establishing branch offices in maternity hospitals to make the process of getting a Social Security number even more convenient!

What's In A Name!

One client who got caught in the ID number net was especially memorable. Mrs. H. claimed three dependents on her return each year. They all had double names, like "Mary Elizabeth," "Billy Bob," and "John Jacob." One year, Mrs. H. came in for her tax appointment and informed me she had lost Mary Elizabeth. I was appalled and immediately asked how it had happened. She replied that Mary Elizabeth had been playing in the front yard and ran after a ball in the street and was hit by a car in the process. I expressed my heartfelt sympathy. Somehow, in our ensuing mutual commiseration, the subject of the funeral came up. Mrs. H. told me that they had buried Mary Elizabeth in the backyard. Once again, I was appalled and commented that I didn't realize it was possible to do that. Mrs. H. kind of shrugged her shoulders, and we moved on to another topic.

A few months later, Mrs. H. was contacted by the IRS: she had omitted providing her dependents' social security numbers on her return. Then—and only then—did I find out that her dependents were ineligible for social security numbers. They were dogs. I should have had a clue.

Confessions of a Tax Accountant

A FEW OF MY FAVORITE DEDUCTIONS

The Spouting Cupids

Not too many people can deduct medical expenses any longer since there is a floor limitation which must be exceeded before any expense is tax deductible. It's a high floor—more than 7 1/2 % of your adjusted gross income. Therefore, for most people covered by medical insurance, no medical deduction is available.

However, what if your doctor prescribes swimming as a prescription for a physical ailment? Could you buy a swimming pool/and or hot tub and deduct it? In most cases, the *amount* of the expense is certainly big enough to exceed the 7 1/2 % floor. The answer to this question is still "maybe. "

Let me tell you about a lady who was a paraplegic. There was no question that she had a medical reason for installing a swimming pool. Her physician had prescribed it, and her condition was serious enough to warrant it. However, the swimming pool cost $100,000. It had been designed to complement her $2 million Gothic Tudor home, and it came complete with spouting cupids.

The tax rule in regard to capital expenditures, i.e. improvements to the home for medical reasons, is that you can deduct only the amount that exceeds the increase in market value to your home. If, for example, if you install a $45,000 swimming pool, and it increases the fair market value of your home by $15,000, then the amount available as a medical deduction would be $30,000. Presumably, the other $15,000 will be reimbursed to you as a part of the sales price of the home when you sell it.

So, what about our lady of the spouting cupids? She took a deduction on her return for the full $100,000 and that amount did raise eyebrows at the IRS.

Upon auditing her return, the IRS disallowed all but about $20,000. Their contention was that she needed only a "bare bones" swimming pool for medical reasons, and the IRS couldn't care less about the aesthetics of her home. (No surprise here.)

Unfortunately for the IRS, our lady took them to Court. The tax court determined that the fair market value of her home had been increased by approximately $30,000, so they allowed her $70,000 as a deduction, less another $5,000 for the cupids.

Although this was good news for the lady, you should swim carefully in this area. There must be a legitimate medical need for swimming pools and hot tubs in order to win in an IRS audit. Remember to watch out for IRS sharks in your swimming pool!

The Well-endowed Girlfriend

Cosmetic surgery is no longer deductible. There was a period of approximately 12 years during the late '70s and early '80s, however, when it was. I recall the year it first became available as a deduction—1976—because I had a lady client who came in that year and asked me very timidly well into the interview if cosmetic surgery was a deductible medical expense. I told her that she was in luck as this was the first year that the deduction was available. All this time, I was carefully looking her over, trying to figure out what part of her anatomy had been surgically improved. Having never been shy, I finally just came out and asked her. I got more of an answer than I had bargained for!

It seems that during the previous summer, she and her husband had attended his 25th-year high school reunion in a distant state. While at the reunion, her husband had renewed his relationship with an old girlfriend who was very well endowed physically. The renewal of the relationship actually resulted in his leaving his wife and moving back to his hometown to marry his high school sweetheart. My client, the abandoned flat-chested spouse, decided to fight fire with fire and invest in silicone implants. In fact, after relating this story to me, she closed the door to my office and showed me her investment.

By now, you may have noticed that being a tax accountant is far from boring work!

The Collection Plate

One other deduction still available to everyone is contributions to a "50l(c)(3) organization." "50l(c)(3)" is tax talk for a section of the Internal Revenue Code that defines the qualifying organization to which you may make tax deductible contributions. Usually these are religious, educational, scientific, or governmental agencies that have a mission to serve the general public. Generally, if you're audited on contributions, the IRS wants to see your cancelled checks or receipts to verify the claimed amount.

Several years ago, one gentleman client of mine was audited on his church donations and duly presented his cancelled checks to the auditor. The amounts were quite large. Although the client had the verification, the IRS auditor somehow smelled a rat, because he followed up with a phone call to the church in question. The minister of the church verified that the checks were indeed accurate, as this particular parishioner was a coin collector who every Sunday bought all the coins that had been deposited in the collection plates!

Valuable Junk

Many organizations accept donations of personal property as well as cash. The deduction allowable for property given away is the fair market value of that property—*on the date you give it away.* The valuations placed on this property can sometimes be questionable and create problems if you are audited. Donations made to organizations such as Goodwill and the Salvation Army usually consist of junk you don't want anymore. You place your own value on this junk since the organizations do not do this. You are supposed to assign a value that approximates what you could sell the item for at a garage sale. Frankly, as a tax accountant, I can tell you that if people thought that they could really get the amounts that they're claiming as the value of their donations, most of them *would* have garage sales and really sell the stuff!

Good record keeping in this area is essential for backing up large deductions. A recent audit of one of my clients was a case in point. He had bought a new home and all new furnishings for it. The old home was sold. After he gave all the good stuff to his kids, he loaded up a truck of what was left—the junk—and donated it to the Goodwill. For this junk, he claimed a deduction of $10,000.

Now, this particular client was an engineer by trade. In my experience, generally my engineer clients are detail-oriented people—they'd like me to include the cents on their tax returns, instead of rounding off to the nearest dollar. This passion for particulars makes for great record keeping. When he was audited, the engineer presented his auditor with a computer printout from his spread-sheet program on his PC that was about a foot thick. It detailed each and every item donated; when he bought it; its condition and age at the time of donation; and its approximate value. There were literally pages and pages and pages ....The auditor took one look and said "Looks okay to me." No fool he.

Confessions of a Tax Accountant

The African Artifact

In this same vein, a client recently wanted to deduct $1,500 for a stuffed elephant he had acquired while on safari in Africa. He had since donated it to Goodwill. I inquired why he would want to give away such an expensive object. (But I was really wondering whether a stuffed elephant could be worth $1,500). He looked at me very seriously and explained, "Well, you see, we had him on display in our living room, and, well—-he began to smell."

We reduced the amount of the donation to a slightly smaller amount.

Once A Mother, Always A Mother

Casualty losses are also deductible on Form 1040, Schedule A, as itemized deductions. But as with medical expenses, in order to deduct a casualty loss, it must exceed 10% of your adjusted gross income. Of course, this means that you must suffer a major disaster in your life to avail yourself of this deduction. Unfortunately, we have had a few of these in the United States in recent years. To name a few, there was the 1989 California earthquake and 1991-1992 hurricanes and tornadoes in Florida and Kauai, and most recently the floods in the Midwest.

During the tax season following the 1989 earthquake in California, one of my clients came in and related the following story:

She was from the Santa Cruz area of California, which was very heavily damaged by the earthquake, and her home had been almost completely destroyed. The day after the quake, she was standing on her property next to her devastated home by the only thing still standing, her fireplace. The media out in force that day happened to pass by her property, noticed her, and asked for an interview. This particular media van happened to be from the "Today" show, and she was interviewed for the following morning's program. This lady's mother, who resided in South Carolina, happened to catch the "Today" show the next morning and saw her daughter on TV amidst the total chaos and destruction of what had been her home. She called her daughter immediately. The first words out of her mouth? "My Gawd, Carol, when are you all going to do something with your hair!?"

Mothers have their priorities . . .

Confessions of a Tax Accountant

A Fishy Story

Recently, a former client of mine was telling me about his trip to Alaska with his wife. The wife caught a 242-pound halibut, which is a very large fish indeed.

The couple was not sure what to do with the fish but after some thought decided to donate it to the Salvation Army in California.

As you may know, taxpayers may take a tax deduction for gifts to charity. If the gift is other than cash, then the amount of the gift is determined by its value at the date of the gift.

My former client, sought the advice of an expert. He contacted the local fishmonger in California and found that at that time halibut was selling for $7.99 per pound.

That halibut gained 500 pounds on its trip from Alaska to San Jose, and the taxpayers tell me that the tax deduction was so large that it saved enough tax to pay for the trip to Alaska.

Ancient Greece

The category called "Miscellaneous Itemized Deductions" used to be a great catch-all for claiming certain employee business expenses, tax preparation fees, investment expenses, safe deposit boxes, and the like. Since 1986, it has only been possible to deduct expenses that exceed a floor of 2% of Adjusted Gross Income. Yep, just as with medical and casualty losses. Trying to be helpful, I offered to raise my fees so that they exceeded 2% of my clients' AGI, but for some reason the idea was not well received by my clientele . . .

Educational expenses used to be deductible in this category as well if the education was directly related to your work and was undertaken to improve skills on the job. Travel as a form of education entered into this category prior to 1986. During this time period, I had an English teacher client who wanted to deduct her trip to Greece, because it was the birthplace of Homer. Those were the days! Pity, they are no more.

MONKEY BUSINESS

As mentioned previously, since 1986 and the Tax Reform Act passed that year, employees have had a tough time deducting expenses related to their employment. These would generally be expenses such as automobile costs, travel and entertainment, or maybe even a computer. These expenses must exceed 2% of their adjusted gross income to be deductible and then it is *only the amount over 2% that is allowed.* Therefore, most of the time, expenses must be reasonably large to be deductible, and since many employees are reimbursed by their employers for major expenses, generally they have nothing to claim. The only remaining alternative for writing off these exciting expenditures is on Schedule C, the form for self-employment. There are no percentage limitations on this form; all legitimate business expenses are deductible. In my experience, a lot of bodies are buried in Schedule C!

The Case of The Disappearing Dogs

For years, I prepared the tax return of a husband and wife who sold dachshunds as their business. They seemed to make a good living doing so, but I must admit I had my doubts as to how anyone could make $30,000 or $40,000 a year selling dogs! Then, five years ago, this client was audited. To my surprise and relief, they received a clean bill of health from the IRS. So you can imagine my chagrin when last year this client was arrested for drug dealing. The dachshund business was a cover-up for the illegal undercover activity. Of course, the drug profits were far more than the $30,000 or $40,000 a year the client had been reporting.

Tax Talk

Many clients have side businesses that they report on Schedule C. Sometimes, they are very unsophisticated about the tax terminology on the government forms. One of the questions asked concerns the accounting method you are using; you must indicate whether you use the cash or accrual method of accounting. This kind of question is obviously a highly technical tax and accounting issue that the average lay person doesn't really understand. I was talking to a client about this recently. I asked him if he was on the cash method of accounting. He replied, "Is that how you CPAs describe living 'hand-to-mouth'?" Another client, when asked about his inventory on a client questionnaire —a number is called for—filled in the word "garage"— that's *where* he stored his inventory—and under method of accounting, he filled in, you guessed it—"calculator." Somehow or other, we get these tax returns done each year!

Tax Deductible Child Birth

Many clients are creative in coming up with business deductions. Years ago, in one of my first years in the business of tax preparation, I encountered a lady who gave instruction in her home on the Lamaze method of child birth. She felt that since she had a bunch of women each week lying on her family room floor practicing child birth that the cost of her carpet should be written off owing to wear and tear. I didn't argue with her.

Confessions of a Tax Accountant

The Human Doughnut Machine

Another question on Schedule C concerns personal consumption in regard to products sold by the self-employed individual. You are supposed to list the total amount of purchases of product on Schedule C and then subtract whatever you used or kept for personal use. I'll never forget the client with the doughnut shop. Evidently, the IRS thought he was eating more doughnuts himself than he was 'fessing' up to. The IRS wanted him to prove how many doughnuts he ate per day/per week/ annualized for the whole year. Yep, taxpayer money was spent on trying to make this thin man confess to having been a doughnut nut!

"The Bluebird of Happiness"

Another very creative client was a doctor in private practice who bought himself a Bluebird Bus for approximately $200,000. This vehicle is what one might call a very upscale RV. The first thing he thought of was how to deduct the new purchase. As it happened, at the time of the purchase he was doing some special surgeries at a remote hospital some distance away from his regular practice. When he performed those surgeries, he had to stay overnight to check on his patients the next day. He didn't like to rely on the sole local motel, as he couldn't reserve in advance. So he would park his "Bluebird" in the hospital parking lot and sleep in it. In addition to this business usage of his bus, Dr. X drove it to Florida for a tax-shelter seminar during the year in question and he claimed this as a business usage of the bus as well. Of course, he didn't invest in the tax shelter, but as you now know, this wasn't so bad. But, unfortunately, the IRS wasn't buying the trip as a business-related expense. However, when Dr. X eventually ended up in tax court over his rather large deduction for the bus, he did get to count the overnighters at the hospital. And since the tax-shelter conference and the surgeon's overnighters were virtually the only uses of the bus that year, Dr. X got a very large tax deduction.

Some of you may know that there are limitations on the amount of depreciation that may be claimed in any one year on luxury vehicles. The target for these limitations, however, is really luxury autos. There is a prominent exception to the rules for vehicles that weigh over 6000 pounds, which the "Bluebird Bus" did. This is a tax example of turning water into wine, transforming personal non-deductible expenses into legal tax deductions for business.

"The Workaholic CPA"

The IRS tries to hold accountants to a higher standard when they audit our tax returns. After all, we're supposed to know what we're doing! So the IRS was more than delighted with one of my compatriots who tried to be creative on his own behalf and got shot down.

CPA Dave was employed full-time at a large accounting firm and during tax season also worked for private clients out of his home. Altogether, he was putting in eighty hours per week. In order to keep up his stamina, he felt it was necessary to belong to a health club and exercise at home when he didn't have time to make it to the club. Naturally, he'd need a home gym. Because he needed stamina to keep up with his workload, he deducted his health club dues and exercise equipment as business expenses.

I'm not sure he slept—and maybe he didn't—because he made no tax deduction for a bed that year. Yet, presumably, sleep is also necessary to keep up one's stamina . . .

The Little Business That Could

Among accountants, some home businesses are notorious for reporting a small amount of income and very large deductions that greatly exceed their income. These businesses sell soap and other household products. I'm never sure who's buying the product, but the expense involved covers the gamut. Typically, there's personal, automobile, large travel and entertainment costs, and an office in the home. The government has recently come out with a new Schedule C EZ, which is supposed to be easier to use than regular Schedule C.

Taxpayers can use it if their gross income is under $25,000, but here's the kicker: expenses must be less than $2,000. The joke among tax accountants is that soap sellers are SOL (sorry, out of luck) for using this form. Their expenses would never be less than $2,000. The reverse is more likely to be usually true—under $2,000 of income and almost

$25,000 in expenses! The idea here, of course, is to make your own business your personal tax shelter.

Understandably, Schedule Cs like this have a high profile and are likely to be audited. Better have all your eggs in a row to prove that your expenses really relate to business and that they are ordinary and necessary in a business like yours.

Confessions of a Tax Accountant

Are We Having Fun Yet?

Businesses are supposed to report income and expense on Form Schedule C. Sometimes, there's a fine line between what's a business and what's a hobby. Businesses are roughly distinguished from hobbies by being undertakings characterized as having an intent to make a profit, but sometimes it's hard to distinguish between the two. This often happens when something fun is involved such as horse breeding or racing, auto racing, or farming, particularly "gentleman" farming, which is usually not the person's main business. Generally, since an argument can be made on both sides of the question, if challenged by the IRS, the final determination will be based on the facts and circumstances of each case, using nine factors that the IRS outlines in their regulations. Note: There is a presumption in this area that if you don't make a profit in 3 out of 5 years you are automatically pursuing a hobby. If your business is determined to be a hobby, you don't get to deduct any losses, but are allowed deductions only to the extent of your income. But this is a presumption that may be rebutted by facts and circumstances. Some people are able to present their case successfully to overcome IRS objections. I've got a winner and a loser that I'd like to tell you about.

Confessions of a Tax Accountant

The Barefoot Stockbroker

My favorite story of recent years having to do with hobbies concerns an ex-commodity broker who got burned out in his hectic profession. He evidently had a mid-life crisis and moved to Hawaii to farm jojoba beans. He had losses for seven straight years. But the court allowed him his losses, because it was very impressed with the fact that a man of his professional background was actually out there in the fields getting his fingernails dirty. The IRS figured he'd only do that if he was in it for a profit.

The "Racy Dentist"

There was "our guy of the cavities" who deducted $27,000 in expenses relating to a cross country racing event for vintage automobiles. He *said* he had a profit motive: the prize was $100,000 if you came in first.

However, he neglected to mention that even if he won, after his spouse, partner and ex-wife took their cuts, only $10,000 would be left for him. Obviously, from the outset, the race would be a losing proposition, not engaged in to make a profit. By the way, he had never raced a vintage automobile before. This guy would meet my definition of an optimist! He met the IRS definition of a hobbyist: deduction denied!

BORN FREE, TAXED TO DEATH

Unfortunately, it's not even possible to die without taxes being a consideration. There's another whole area of tax law that concerns estates and gifts which differs from income tax law but is no less painful. The only good thing is that with your estate tax, you're no longer around to feel the pain.

Confessions of a Tax Accountant

Florida Sunset

One recent "dearly departed" left quite a mess for his heirs. He was a pilot who one fateful evening flew from Kentucky to Florida on what turned out to be an illegal—and fatal—mission.

In Florida, he ran into an electrical storm which downed his small plane and left him dead but his cargo intact. His cargo was about 600 pounds of marijuana. The marijuana was immediately confiscated by the authorities at the scene of the crash.

Under both Kentucky and Florida law, you own property if you're in possession of it at the time of your death. Therefore, the marijuana cache was included by the IRS in the pilot's gross estate at street value. His heirs had to pay estate tax on this asset, even though it had been confiscated by authorities.

There must be a moral to this story! "The wages of sin will be visited unto the last generation?"

"War and Peace"

And then there was the World War II vet who died some years ago in Texas. At the time of his death, his heirs did not file an estate tax return because, according to them, his assets were less than $600,000. (This is the amount of the estate tax exemption; if you leave less than $600,000 in assets, there is no estate tax.)

However, several years later, it came to the attention of the IRS that there might be more to this story. It seems that the deceased had been stationed in Germany right after the war and had had access to some of the antiquities, artifacts, and works of art that had been collected by the Nazi regime. He systematically stole everything he could get his hands on and shipped it home to mama, who, by the way, was an art professor.

All of these very valuable treasures were stored in bank vaults in the G.I.'s hometown. At the time of the vet's death, various family member were aware of the "goods." They laid low for two or three years after his death and then contacted an attorney in Switzerland through whom the vet had evidently sold things. The heirs arranged to sell one of the art works for three million dollars. The plot thickened when the prospective buyer, a cathedral in Germany, recognized the artwork as one that had been stolen from it during the war. The cathedral's representatives proceeded to hire a detective to determine the identity of the seller. The detective traced the culprit back to Texas, and the whole story began to unfold.

In addition to having to deal with the cathedral's claims, the heirs now also had trouble with the IRS. It seems that the estate was quite a bit larger than $600,000. The government's position in this case is that all of the stolen goods should be included in the gross estate of the deceased. This was judged to amount to several *million* dollars. Of course, the heirs are crying foul and appealing the IRS decision. After all, *they* weren't thieves! But they felt quite comfortable with the idea of raking in the proceeds from selling stolen goods. Will justice rule the day? What is justice?

CONFESSIONS OF A TAX ACCOUNTANT

My Clients—It Takes All Sorts

In the introduction, I mentioned that psychology has come in handy in my business. Client behavior is all over the map, reflecting unique psyches. But once I figure out where a client is coming from, I know what to expect from year to year and how to deal with him or her.

Some clients—*not* my most favorite—are nit pickers. Every detail must be *exactly* right or my work will be deemed unacceptable. They are one extreme. At the other, are the "broad brush stroke artists" who want me to "gin something up" for their signature! When I interview such a client, I might ask, "What were your donations for this year?" Response: "What did I claim last year?" Translation: "Put down what I claimed last year, plus 10% for inflation and general principles!"

Some clients have impeccable records, some have none. The same people come in for their appointments at the same time every year. The same people file on extension every year. I even have a small group of clients who file only every three years, when the government gets nasty with them and sends unpleasant greetings. Usually, these people *really* hate taxes; they can't stand to do them and would put it off forever, if the long arm of the IRS were not menacing them.

Confessions of a Tax Accountant

Tax Revenge of The Wronged Spouse

Speaking of the long arm, the IRS has a policy of rewarding people who provide information on cheaters. Taxtale tellers get something like 10% of the amount collected due to a snitch's information. In my career, I have only twice talked to a client about this possibility. The first was an ex-husband who was paying a great deal of alimony to his ex-wife. Alimony is tax deductible to the payer and is included as income of the payee. The IRS now tracks alimony by requiring spouses who deduct it to include the ID number on their tax return of the spouse collecting it. But years ago, this wasn't the case. Sometime during that era, an ex-husband client came in for his tax appointment and was lamenting the fact that he was paying his ex-spouse all these thousands of dollars and he was just sure that she was not reporting the income on her tax return. I mentioned to him the IRS "snitch" program, and he kind of leaned back in his chair.

You could actually see the wheels going around in his head. Finally, he said to me: "You know, I've really given this a lot of thought, but I hate the IRS even more than I hate my ex-wife!"

Confessions of a Tax Accountant

The Handicapped Golfer

More recently, I had a client who was a member of a nearby country club where for many years he played golf almost daily. One day, out of the blue, I got a phone call from him asking me about the tax reporting requirements for such an organization. He was convinced that they needed to be filing tax returns to report the dues and collections from various golf tournaments and he wanted to report them to IRS for not doing so. He obviously had a bee in his bonnet. He'd been a member of this organization for years. Why would he now want to turn in his fellow duffers? It finally developed that they had lowered his golf handicap by a stroke, because he was winning all the tournaments. Hell hath no fury like a golfer with a lowered handicap!

The Accountant's Ego

I have found that I play a big part in peoples' lives through helping them make important financial decisions. And as noted in these pages, sometimes that leads to talking to my clients about other important parts of their lives.

For example, I had an elderly client (mid-80s) come in to see me this year. She is not greatly wealthy, but she's certainly well off, with enough money to live out her life comfortably and then some. I asked her if she had taken a vacation recently. No, she hadn't; she didn't think that she could afford any more vacations, because she would have to take the money out of principal and she didn't think she should touch her principal. In my view, this lady could clearly afford to use principal without jeopardizing her future, and I told her so. I also mentioned to her that as far as I knew, most of us only go around once . . . . She immediately brightened up and left my office intending to plan a trip. All she needed was my "okay." I don't think that the same advice coming from a family member would have been as convincing.

A married couple of mine have very different ideas of how, when, and where they should retire. He wants to live in their vacation home and sell their primary residence. She wants to stay close to old friends and where medical care is more readily available. At a recent session in my office, I helped them reach a compromise solution.

You may note that none of the above had anything to do with income tax per se!

In tax time, I really am important. I can call clients at their place of work and get through secretaries, receptionists, and sometimes even voice mail just as easily as if "The President" were calling. It's a standing joke that if it's tax time, surgeon clients will take calls in the operating room.

Consider the client of an accountant friend of mine who was thirty minutes late for her tax appointment. She apologized profusely, stating that her husband had died that morning and she had to wait until the coroner came to the house before she could leave for her appointment!

So at least at tax time, we know we're important to people. Most of us realize that we've been chosen to perform a necessary service, not just for our professional expertise, but because our personalities jive with our clients' and our clients have come to trust us.

Confessions of a Tax Accountant

The Referral

Confessions of a Tax Accountant

The best advice I can give to you in choosing a tax accountant besides checking to see if he or she possesses the required credentials is to pick someone you're comfortable working with and believe to be trustworthy.

A favorite story of mine actually came from a comic strip featuring "Rabbit," the bartender, talking to a customer. The customer asked the bartender "Rabbit" to look at his tax return -"the return your accountant did for me." Rabbit replies: "Oh yeah, how'd he do?" Customer: "He committed two felonies, one count of mail fraud, and an act of treason and that's just on the first page." Rabbit's response: "Hey! I told you he was good!"

It used to be that people chose their accountant based on the size of the refund they got for some friend or relative. Of course, that was in the days when people still got refunds!

But a word of warning: Watch out for creative accountants like "Rabbit's." Most of the really creative ones I know are now serving time in minimum security prisons.

A Final Word

Another problem we accountants have is that we're often the messenger of bad news. And we don't want to get shot. We're the visible targets for all the government's foibles—-new complex tax laws, higher marginal rates, bigger bites of paychecks from social security taxes—all things that frustrate our clients. Unlike Congress, as an accountant, I can run, but I can't hide.

Under my green eyeshade, it's been fun, exciting, scary—but never, never, never dull.

I consider tax accounting and tax preparation a very rich profession. Of course, it does involve numbers, but, as you will have realized from my stories, it's very largely a "people profession." It features all kinds of people, with all kinds of foibles and sterling qualities, who, by sharing their life stories, make my work endlessly challenging and fulfilling. Someday, university accounting programs may include a course called "Psychology for Tax Accountants in Everyday Life." It's about time they did!

NOTE: This book is not a technical book on tax preparation and no inferences should be taken from it. Please consult your professional advisor for such information.

Have You Had a Humorous or Interesting Income Tax Experience?

Please send your stories to the publisher for possible inclusion in the author's upcoming sequel "More Confessions." Real names are not used in order to protect the innocent and in some cases the guilty!

Send your stories to: **Canyon View Institute**
11475 Canyon View Circle
Cupertino, California 95014